THE BOOK OF MUSLIM NAMES

MELS

بسم الله الرحمن الرحيم

هُوَ اللَّهُ الْخَالِقُ الْبَارِئُ الْمُصَوِّرُ لَهُ الْأَسْمَاءُ الْحُسْنَىٰ

يُسَبِّحُ لَهُ مَا فِي السَّمَاوَاتِ وَالْأَرْضِ وَهُوَ الْعَزِيزُ الْحَكِيمُ الحشر ٢٤

He is God, the Creator, the Maker Who shapes all
forms and appearances.
His are the most beautiful names.
All that is in the heavens and the earth
extols his limitless glory
and He is the Mighty, the Wise.

(*Al-Qur'an*, Surah al-Hashr, 59:24)

Published by MELS
Muslim Education & Literary Services, UK
Website: www.melspublications.com
Email: orders@melspublications.com
mels@webstar.co.uk
Freephone: 0800 081 1942

First edition London, 1985
Reprinted 1986, 1990, 1996, 2000, 2004

ISBN 0 984196 03 3

Compilation by Azieza Hamid

Calligraphy by Muhammad F Arovah

Design by Zafar Malik, Umran Design, London

Printed and bound by The Cromwell Press, Trowbridge, Wiltshire

Introduction

The Right to a Beautiful and Honourable Name

Choosing a name for a newcomer to Islam, whether a new-born babe or an adult, is usually a pleasant and exciting exercise. It can also be a difficult one for those who are unsure of the form and meanings of Arabic words in particular.

The selection of a good name is of course one of the first important duties of a parent to a child and should not be treated lightly. According to the Prophet Muhammad, it is a child's *right* to be given a good and honourable name.

What's in a name and what constitutes a good and honourable name?

A person's name, whether it is Muslim or not, usually tells something about the cultural milieu in which he is born and in which he grows up. It gives some indication of his heritage and the values which his parents hold dear. A name like Muhammad ibn Abdul Aziz places its bearer firmly within the mainstream of Muslim civilization. A name like Tom Ahmed is indicative of some form of cultural transformation or indeed of confusion and disorientation.

Names may be chosen for their historical, religious or moral significance or simply because they "sound nice". For historical names in the Islamic tradition, people often turn first of all to the names of the Prophets, may God's peace be with them all. It is proper, according to the Prophet, to give the names of angels and prophets. Prophet Muhammad himself named one of his sons after the Prophet Ibrahim. They also turn to the Companions of the Prophet and other men and women who are known for their virtuous acts or who have made some significant contribution to Muslim civilization. This book features many such names but it has not been possible here to describe who the bearers were or what contribution they made.

Among the best Muslim names are those which describe a relationship between man and his Creator – man as either serving, worshipping, praising, or thanking God as He manifests Himself through His many attributes. The most important set of names in this category are those which begin with 'Abd (عبد) and which are (as they must be) followed by one of the attributes of God. These are listed separately in this book. It is important to bear in mind that a person cannot be named simply by an attribute of God alone but that this attribute must be preceded by the word 'Abd meaning Servant. For instance, a person may not be called Al-Ḥamīd (the Praised One) but 'Abd al-Ḥamīd (Servant of the Praised One). It is also worthwhile pointing out here that "Abdul" is not a word on its own and such names as Abdul Bunga or Abdul Minty are quite nonsensical.

According to the Prophet, peace be upon him, the best of names are 'Abdullah and 'Abdur Rahman.

A great number of names simply represent a virtue which the bearer is expected to live up to. Names abound with meanings such as love and chastity, tenderness and compassion or perseverance and struggle. Names are also derived from the world of natural phenomena, heavenly bodies, animals, birds and flowers although in many cases this is a practice of fairly recent provenance.

Here is not the place to go into the rather fascinating discussion on the names Muslims choose for their children, the names by which we are known or choose to be known and some of the reasons underlying the giving or taking of names. There is of course a very great variety of practices current and it is possible to show that this variety reflects different levels of Islamic consciousness, and the diversity at best or the chaos at worst of the Muslim world.[1]

For our purposes here it is pertinent to state that most Muslim names have an Arabic component. A persons full name may be completely Arabic, or it may be composed of an Arabic first name with a second name from a local language whether it be Turkish, Yoruba, Urdu, Thai, Chinese or English. Whatever the form, it is clearly desirable, even mandatory, to have some knowledge of Arabic and its proper pronunciation if one is to make sense and have a full appreciation of Muslim names. This is especially so bearing in mind the fact that a mere lengthening of a vowel or the thickening of a consonant could radically alter the meaning of a word and may even be blasphemous. For example, the name Hafiz (حافظ) with a long 'a' means successful and can stand on its own. With a short 'a' and a long 'i' (حفيظ) it means Protector and is a Divine name which cannot be used on its own as a person's name. Another example: the name Abd al-Haqq means Servant of God – the Truth. If the heavy sound of the consonant 'Qaf' at the end of al-Haqq is mispronounced as a 'Kaf', one would get the blasphemous name of Abd al-Hakk meaning Servant of Scratching.[2]

It is crucially important then to have Islamic names pronounced accurately. The best way to ensure this is to go directly, in the first instance, to the original

Arabic and not to any of the various forms of spelling and transliteration that are used in English.

The spelling of Arabic names in English does pose certain problems. There is, however, quite an accurate system of transliteration of Arabic into English which involves the use of diacritical marks: a dot below certain consonants to indicate a thick sound; a dash above vowels to indicate long vowels; an open inverted comma (') to represent the letter 'Ayn; and a closed inverted comma (') to represent the Hamza (ء) or the glottal stop. This is the system that has been used in this book. Although it is technically correct, many individuals would find it cumbersome to employ these diacritical marks in the spelling of their names. We therefore suggest below various alternative renderings which could be used.

Long Vowels

In this book, a stroke is placed above the vowels a, i and u to lengthen them. Alternatively,

the long vowel 'a' may also be rendered 'aa';
the long vowel 'i' may also be rendered 'ee' or 'ie'; and
the long vowel 'u' may also be rendered 'oo' or 'ou'.

Examples

1. The word Sājid (ساجد) may be rendered Saajid.
2. The word 'Azīzah' (عزيزة) may be spelt in the following different ways:
   Azeezah
   Aziezah
   Aziza
   Azeeza
   Azieza.
   The open inverted comma in the original transliteration stands for the letter 'Ayn (ع). The 'h' at the end of word stands for the ta' marbutah (ö) which normally indicates a feminine ending. This 'h' should properly be included but is often dropped in English transliterations.
3. The word Mahmud may be rendered as Mahmood or Mahmoud.

Dipthongs

1. The diphthong 'aw' in words like 'Mawdūd' (مودود) may be rendered as 'au' and the word then spelt as 'Maudud'.
2. The diphthong 'ay' in words like'Ruqayyah'(رقية) may be rendered as 'ai' and the word then spelt 'Ruqaiyah'.

Names beginning with ‘Abd (عبد)
A name like ‘Abd al-Wadūd (عبد الودود) may be rendered in the following different ways:

Abdu-l-Wadud
Abdul Wadud
AbdulWadud

Such compound names where the ‘l’ of the definite article ‘al’ is written in Arabic but not pronounced need to be treated differently. A name like ‘Abd ar-Raḥmān (عبد الرحمن) may be rendered alternatively as:

Abdur Rahman
Abdu-r-Rahman
AbdurRahman.

In cases like the above, it may be better to opt for the hyphenated alternative or the name written as one word (which we have done in the text) to avoid Abd or Abdul being treated as a name on its own, a practice which is clearly absurb.

Special Arabic letters

The transliteration of certain Arabic characters (some unique to Arabic) is presented in names in which they occur in the text as follows:

ḥ	ح	ẓ	ظ
kh	خ	‘	ع
dh	ذ	gh	غ
ṣ	ص	q	ق
ḍ	ض	’	ء
ṭ	ط		

Although it may be inconvenient to put the dot or use inverted commas (where they apply) in spelling one’s names, it is important to pronounce these letters correctly as they are sounded in Arabic for the reasons we have mentioned above.

In pronouncing, it is important to differentiate between the letters in each of the following groups of characters.

ا ع	د ض
ت ط	ذ ز ظ
ث س ص	خ ق ك
ح ه	ذ ز ظ

If the above explanations and instructions seem too complicated or difficult to follow, it is recommended that help be sought from someone who knows Arabic in order to obtain the exact pronunciation of a name or to advise on meanings especially when words are combined to form a compound name as is a common practice in certain parts of the Muslim world.

If you are tempted to throw up your hands in despair in choosing a name, do remember that a name is something that one has to live with throughout one's life. The least one can expect is that one's name should be spelt and pronounced properly. It is hoped that this book will be useful in this regard.

الله أكبر ولله الحمد وله الأسماء الحسنى
God is Great. To God is all praise and to Him belongs the most excellent names.

Abdul Wahid Hamid

[1] For such a discussion, see the article on 'Naming' in *The Muslim*, London. vol 12, no. 1, 1974.
[2] For these and other examples see article 'Your Name, the Holy Qur'an and Islam' by Isma'il R Al-Faruqi in *Muslim Names*, American Trust Publications, 1977.

FEMALE NAMES

A

ʻĀbidah عابدة
Worshipper

ʻAbīr عبير
Fragrance, Perfume

ʻAbdah عبدة
Worshipper (of God)

ʻAblah عبلة
■ Perfectly formed

Adībah
■ Literateur, Authoress

ʻĀdilah عادلة
■ Just, Honest

ʻAdīlah عديلة
■ Equal

ʻAfāf عفاف
■ Chastity, Modesty

ʻAfīfah عفيفة
■ Chaste, Modest

ʻĀfiyah عافية
■ Health, Vigour

ʻAfrā’ عفراء
■ Dust-coloured; (One of the first women from Madinah to accept Islam)

Aḥlām أحلام
■ Dreams

ʻĀ’ishah عائشة
■ Living, Prosperous (Wife of Prophet Muhammad)

Akīdah اكيدة
■ Certain, Firm

ʻĀkifah عاكفة
■ Intent, Busy

ʻĀlimah عالمة
■ Woman of learning, Scholar

ʻAlīmah عليمة
■ Well-informed, Learned

ʻĀliyah عالية
■ Elevated, Outstanding

ʻAlīyah علية
■ Exalted, Highest Social Standing

Almās ألماس
■ Diamond

Amal أمل
■ Hope, Aspiration

Āmāl آمال
■ Hopes, Aspirations

Amānī أماني
■ Wishes, Aspirations

Amatullāh أمة الله
■ Servant of God

ʻAmbar عنبر
■ Perfume, Ambergris

ʻAmbrīn عنبرين
■ Of Ambergris

Āmilah آملة
■ Hopeful

Āminah آمنة
■ Safe, Secure, Protected; (Mother of Prophet Muhammad)

Amīnah أمينة
■ Trustworthy, Loyal Custodian

ʻĀmirah عامرة
■ Civilized, Prosperous

Amīrah أميرة
■ Princess, Leader

Anāh أناة
■ Perseverance, Patience

ʻAnān عنان
■ Clouds

ʻAndalah عندلة
■ Song of the Nightingale

ʻAndalīb عندليب
■ Nightingale

Anīqah أنيقة
■ Neat, Elegant

Anīsah أنيسة
■ Friendly, Affectionate; Close Friend

Anwār أنوار
■ Rays of Light

ʻĀqilah عاقلة
■ Sensible, Discerning, Intelligent

‘Aqīlah عقيلة
■ The Best, the Pick

Arīj أريج
■ Fragrance, Sweet Smell

Arījah أريجة
■ Fragrant, Sweet-smelling

‘Arūb عروب
■ Loving

Arwā أروى
■ Mountain Goat

Asīlah أصيلة
■ Of Noble Origin, Authentic, Genuine

‘Āṣimah عاصمة
■ Protector

Āṣirah آصرة
■ Bond

Āsiyah آسية
■ Comforting, Consoling: (Wife of Pharoah)

Asmā’ أسماء
■ Loftier, More Eminent; (Daughter of Abu Bakr)

‘Aṣmā’ عصماء
■ Excellent, Precious

‘Āṭifah عاطفة
■ Affectionate, Compassionate, Sympathetic

‘Aṭīfah عطيفة
■ Affection, Compassion

‘Ātikah عاتكة
■ Clear, Pure

‘Āṭirah عاطرة
■ Fragrant, Aromatic

‘Aṭīyah عطية
■ Gift, Present

‘Awāṭif عواطف
■ Emotions

Azhār أزهار
■ Flowers, Blossoms

‘Azīmah عزيمة
■ Determined; Determination, Firm Will

‘Aẓīmah عظيمة
■ Great, Powerful

‘Azīzah عزيزة
■ Beloved, Dear, Precious

‘Azzah عزة
■ Young Gazelle

B

Badīhah بديهة
Insight, Perceptive Faculty

Badrīyah بدرية
Resembling Full Moon

Bahīj بهيج
Magnificent, Splendid

Bahīrah بهيرة
■ Dazzling, Brilliant

Bahīyah بهية
■ Beautiful, Splendid, Radiant

Bakārah بكارة
■ Virginity

Bakūrah بكورة
■ Precocious

Balīghah بليغة
■ Eloquent

Banān بنان
■ Fingertips

Barī’ah بريئة
■ Innocent

Bāri‘ah بارعة
■ Excelling

Bashīrah بشيرة
■ Bringer of Good News

Bāsilah باسلة
■ Brave, Fearless, Intrepid

Bāsimah باسمة
■ Smiling

Basīmah بسيمة
■ Smiling

Basmah بسمة
■ Smile

Bilqīs بلقيس
- Name of the Queen of Sheba

Bushrā بشرى
- Good news, Glad Tidings

Buthaynah بثينة
- Of beautiful and tender body

D

Dalāl دلال
- Coquetry

Dāliyā دالية
- Dahlia

Dhahabīyah ذهبية
- Golden, Precious

Dhākirah ذاكرة
- One who remembers God

Dhakīyah ذكية
- Bright, Intelligent

Ḍuḥā ضحى
- Brightness, Early Morning

Durrah درة
- Pearl

F

Fāḍilah فاضلة
- Outstanding, Distinguished, Learned

Faḍīlah فضيلة
- Outstanding, Deserving, Erudite; Moral Excellence, Virtue, Merit

Fadwah فدوة
- Derived from self-sacrifice

Fahīmah فهيمة
- Discerning, Intelligent

Fā'idah فائدة
- Benefit, Advantage

Fā'iqah فائقة
- Surpassing, Excellent, Superb

Fā'izah فائزة
- Victorious

Fākhirah فاخرة
- Glorious, Magnificent

Fakhrīyah فخرية
- Honorary, Proud; Glory, Pride

Fakhrun-Nisā' فخر النساء
- Pride of Women (Famous Muslim writer)

Faqīhah فقيهة
- Expert, Understanding

Faraḥ فرح
- Joy, Cheerfulness

Farḥānah فرحانة
- Joyful, Delighted

Farīdah فريدة
- Unique, Precious, Gem

Fariḥah فرحة
- Lively, Comely

Farīḥah فريحة
- Happy, Joyful

Farwah فروة
- Fur; (Daughter of Imam Ja'far as-Sadiq)

Faṣīḥah فصيحة
- Eloquent

Fāṭimah فاطمة
- Weaning (Daughter of the Prophet)

Fātinah فاتنة
- Intelligent, Charming, Fascinating

Fawḥah فوحة
- Breath of Fragrance

Fawzah فوزة
- Success, Triumph

Fawzīyah فوزية
- Successful

Fayrūz فيروز
- Turquoise

Firdaws فردوس
- Paradise, Garden

Fukayhah فكيهة
■ Proper Name
(Early Muslim convert)

G

Ghādah غادة
Beautiful

Ghaydā' غيداء
Young, Delicate

Ghāliyah غالية
Valuable, Dear, Beloved
Perfume from musk and ambergris

Ghazālah غزالة
■ Gazelle

Ghāzīyah غازية
■ Fighter

Ghuṣūn غصون
■ Branches (of a tree)

H

Ḥabībah حبيبة
Beloved

Hādiyah هادية
Calm, Tranquil;
Guide to righteousness

Hadīyah هدية
Gift

Ḥāfiẓah حافظة
■ Successful

Ḥafīẓah حفيظة
■ Guardian

Ḥafṣah حفصة
■ Cub;
(Wife of the Prophet Muhammad)

Hājar هاجر
■ Wife of Prophet Ibrahim

Hājirah هاجرة
■ Migrant

Ḥakīmah حكيمة
■ Wise, Judicious

Hālah هالة
■ Aureole

Ḥalīmah حليمة
■ Gentle, Clement

Ḥāmidah حامدة
■ Praising (God), Appreciative

Ḥamīdah حميدة
■ Praiseworthy, Commendable, Praised

Ḥamīmah حميمة
■ Close friend

Ḥammādah حمادة
■ Praising (God)

Hanā' هناء
■ Bliss, Felicity

Ḥannah حنة
■ Sympathy, Compassion

Ḥannān حنان
■ Affectionate, Loving, Tender

Ḥanīfah حنيفة
■ True (believer), Upright

Ḥanīn حنين
■ Longing, Yearning

Hāni'ah هانئة
■ Happy, Delighted

Hanī'ah هنيئة
■ Pleasant, Agreeable, Wholesome

Ḥarīr حرير
■ Silk

Ḥaṣīfah حصيفة
■ Endowed with sound judgment

Ḥasīnah حسينة
■ Pretty, Beautiful

Ḥasnā' حسناء
■ Beautiful, A Beauty

Ḥawwā' حواء
■ Eve

Ḥayā' حياء
■ Modesty, Shyness

Ḥayāh حياة
■ Life

Hayfā' هيفاء
- Slender, of Beautiful Body

Hibah هبة
- Gift, Present

Hibatullāh هبة الله
- Gift of God

Ḥikmah حكمة
- Wisdom

Hind هند
- Proper Name

Hudā هدى
- Guidance

Ḥumayrā' حميراء
- Epithet given by the Prophet Muhammad to his wife A'ishah

Hurayrah هريرة
- Kitten

Ḥūrīyah حورية
- Virgin of Paradise

Ḥurrīyah حرية
- Freedom, Liberty

Ḥusn حسن
- Beauty

Ḥusnā حسنى
- Most Beautiful

I

Ibrisām ابرسام
Silk

Ibrīz إبريز
Pure Gold

Ibtihāj إبتهاج
Delight, Joy

Ibtihāl إبتهال
- Supplication, Prayer

Ibtisām إبتسام
- Smile

'Iffah عفة
- Purity, Modesty

Ilḥām إلهام
- Inspiration, Intuition

Imān إيمان
- Faith, Belief

Imtithāl إمتثال
- Polite Obedience

In'ām انعام
- Act of Kindness, Benefaction

Īnās ايناس
- Sociability, Geniality

'Ināyah عناية
- Concern, Solicitude

Istabraq إستبرق
- Brocade

Izdihār إزدهار
- Flourishing, Blossoming

J

Jabīn جبين
Forehead

Jalā' جلاء
Clarity, Elucidation

Jalīlah جليلة
Splendid, Significant

Jamīlah جميلة
- Beautiful, Elegant, Graceful

Janān جنان
- Heart, Soul

Jannah جنة
- Heaven, Paradise

Jawāhir, جواهر
- Precious Stones, Jewels

Jawharah جوهرة
- Jewel, Gem

Jumānah جمانة
- Silver Pearl

Junaynah جنينة
- Little Garden

Juwayrīyah جويرية
- Wife of Prophet Muhammad

K

Kabīrah كبيرة
Great

Kāmilah كاملة
Complete, Perfect

Karam كرم
Noble Nature

Karīmah كريمة
■ Generous, Noble

Kāshifah كاشفة
■ Discoverer

Kawthar كوثر
■ Abundance; River in Paradise

Khadījah خديجة
■ Wife of Prophet Muhammad

Khālidah خالدة
■ Eternal, Glorious

Khalīlah خايلة
■ Friend

Khāliṣah خالصة
■ Pure, Clear

Khansā' خنساء
■ Proper Name (Famous Arabic poetess)

Khaṭībah خطيبة
■ Orator, Speaker

Khawlah خولة
■ Proper Name

Khayrīyah خيرية
■ Charitable, Good

Khuzāmah خزامة
■ Lavender

Kubrā كبرى
■ Great, Senior (Al-Kubra – epithet of Khadijah)

L

Labībah
Understanding, Sensible, Intelligent

Lā'iqah
Suitable, Deserving, Elegant

Lamīsah لميسة
■ Soft to the touch

Lamyā' لمياء
■ Dark-lipped

Laṭīfah لطيفة
■ Kind, Gentle, Refined

Laylā ليلى
■ Proper Name

Layyinah لينة
■ Tender, Supple, Resilient

Līnā لينا
■ Tender

Lubābah لبابة
■ The Innermost essence

Luṭfīyah لطفية
■ Delicate, Graceful

M

Madanīyah مدنية
Civilized, Urbane, Polished

Madīḥah مديحة
Praise, Commendation; Praiseworthy, Commendable

Maḥbūbah محبوبة
■ Beloved

Maḥfūẓah محفوظة
■ Protected

Maḥmūdah محمودة
■ Praised, Commendable

Majdah مجدة
■ Glory, Nobility

Majdīyah مجدية
■ Glorious

Mājidah ماجدة
■ Glorious, Noble, Respected

Majīdah مجيدة
■ Sublime

Malak ملك
■ Angel

Malikah ملكة
■ Queen

Mālikah مالكة
■ Reigning, Ruling

Malīkah مليكة
■ Queen

Manāl منال
■ Attainment, Achievement

Manṣūrah منصورة
■ Supporter, Victorious

Marām مرام
■ Aspiration

Marḍīyah مرضية
■ Commendable, Pleasing (to God)

Mariḥah مرحة
■ Joyful, Cheerful, Lively

Marghūbah مرغوبة
■ Coveted, Desired

Ma'rūfah معروفة
■ Known, Accepted; Benefit

Maryam مريم
■ Name of mother of Jesus

Masrurah مسرورة
■ Glad, Happy, Delighted

Mastūrah مستورة
■ Latent, Hidden, Chaste

Mas'ūdah مسعودة
■ Happy, Fortunate

Ma'ṣūmah معصومة
■ Innocent

Mawāhib مواهب
■ Talents

Māwiyah ماوية
■ Old Arabic Name

Maymūnah ميمونة
■ Fortunate, Blessed; (Wife of Prophet Muhammad)

Maysā' ميساء
■ Walking with a proud, swinging gait

Maysūn ميسون
■ Of Beautiful face and body

Mayyādah ميادة
■ Walking with a swinging gait

Mazīyah مزية
■ Excellence, Merit, Virtue

Mu'aẓẓamah معظمة
■ Respected, Exalted

Mubārakah مباركة
■ Blessed, Auspicious

Mubīnah مبينة
■ Clear, Evident, Plain

Mufīdah مفيدة
■ Favourable, Useful

Muhjah مهجة
■ Lifeblood, heart, Soul

Muḥṣanah محصنة
■ Protected, Sheltered, Chaste

Muḥsinah محسنة
■ Charitable, Benevolent; Benefactor

Mujāhidah مجاهدة
■ Struggler, Fighter

Mujībah مجيبة
■ Respondent, Answering

Mukarramah مكرمة
■ Honoured, Revered

Mukhliṣah مخلصة
■ Devoted, Faithful, Pure-hearted

Mu'minah مؤمنة
■ Faithful; Believer

Munā منى
■ Wish, Desire

Munawwarah منورة
■ Radiant, Illuminated

Munībah منيبة
■ Repentant

Munīrah منيرة
■ Brilliant, Illuminating

Munnah منة
■ Strength, Vigour

Muqaddasah مقدسة
■ Sacred, Holy

Murīḥah مريحة
■ Restful, Soothing

Murshidah مرشدة
■ Woman Guide, Guide

Muṣaddiqah مصدقة
■ One who affirms the Truth

Musharrafah مشرفة
■ Honoured, Elevated

Mushīrah مشيرة
■ Giving Counsel, Advising

Muṭahharah مطهرة
■ Purified, Chaste

N

Nabīhah نبيهة
■ Noble, Eminent

Nabīlah نبيلة
■ Noble, Magnanimous

Nadā ندى
■ Generosity; Dew

Naḍhīrah نذيرة
■ Warner

Nadīdah نديدة
■ Equal, Rival

Nadīmah نديمة
■ Friend

Nāḍirah ناضرة
■ Flourishing, Radiant

Naḍīrah نضيرة
■ Flourishing, Radiant

Nādirah نادرة
■ Rare, Precious

Nādiyah نادية
■ Caller, Announcer

Naḍrah نضرة
■ Bloom, Glamour

Nafīsah نفيسة
■ Precious, Delicate; gem

Nāhiḍah ناهضة
■ Elevated, Dilligent

Naḥlah نحلة
■ Bee

Nā'ilah نائلة
■ Winner, Earner; A Boon

Nā'imah ناعمة
■ Enjoying the bounty of God

Na'īmah نعيمة
■ Smooth, Tender

Najdah نجدة
■ Courage, Bravery

Najah نجاة
■ Success, Safety

Najībah نجيبة
■ Noble, Distinguished

Nājiyah ناجية
■ Safe

Najlā' نجلاء
■ Of wide Eyes

Najmah نجمة
■ Star

Najwā نجوى
■ Confidential talk, Romantic

Naqībah نقيبة
■ Leader, Head

Naqīyah نقية
■ Pure, Clean, Clear

Nashā نشا
■ Scent, Perfume

Nashwā نشوى
■ Elated, Exultant, Flushed

Nashwah نشوة
■ Fragrance, Aroma

Nāṣifah ناصفة
■ Just, Equitable

Nāṣiḥah ناصحة
■ Advisor; Sincere

Nasīmah نسيمة
■ Gentle breeze, zephyr

Nāṣirah ناصرة
■ Helper, Protector

Naṣīrah نصيرة
■ Supporter, Defender

Nawāl نوال
■ Gift

Nawār نوار
■ Blossom, Flower

Nazāhah نزاهة
■ Purity, Righteousness, Honesty

Nāzihah نازهة
■ Pure, Honest

Nazīhah نزيهة
■ Honest

Nāẓimah ناظمة
■ Arranger, Organizer; Poetess

Nāẓirah ناظرة
■ Observer, Supervisor

Naẓīrah نظيرة
■ Like, Equal, Matching

Nidā' نداء
■ Call

Niḥāl نحال
■ Presents, Gifts

Niḥlah نحلة
■ Present, Gift

Ni'mah نعمة
■ Blessing, Favour

Nuḍār نضار
■ Gold

Nuhā نهى
■ Intelligent

Nūrānīyah نورانية
■ Luminous, Brilliant

Nūrīyah نورية
■ Radiant, Brilliant

Nusaybah نسيبة
■ Proper Name
(One of the first women of Madinah to accept Islam)

Q

Qābilah قابلة
Able, Wise

Qādirah قادرة
Powerful, Able

Qāhirah قاهرة
Overpowering, Victorious

Qudsīyah قدسية
■ Glorious, Sacred

Qurratu-l 'Ayn قرة العين
■ Delight of the Eye, Darling

R

Rabāb رباب
White Cloud
(Wife of Husayn – grandson of the Prophet)

Rābi'ah رابعة
Fourth
(Name of Rabi'ah al-Adawiyah)

Rabī'ah ربيعة
■ Garden

Rāḍiyah راضية
■ Satisfied, Content

Raḍwā رضوى
■ Name of Mountain in Madinah

Rafā' رفاء
■ Happiness, Prosperity

Rafī'ah رفيعة
■ High, Sublime, Exquisite

Rafīqah رفيقة
■ Friend, Companion

Raghd رغد
■ Pleasure

Rāghibah راغبة
■ Desiring, Desirous

Rāḥah راحة
■ Rest, Comfort

Rāḥīl راحيل
■ Rachel

Raḥīmah رحيمة
■ Kind, Compassionate

Raḥmah رحمة
■ Compassion, Mercy: (Wife of Prophet Ayyub)

Rā'idah رائدة
■ Leader, Pioneer

Ra'iḥah رائحة
■ Fragrance, Perfume

Ra'īmah رئيمة
■ Loving tenderly

Ra'īsah رئيسة
■ Leader, Matron

Rā'īyah راعية
■ Shepherdess

Rājiyah راجية
■ Hoping, Full of hope

Ramlah رملة
■ Proper Name; (Real Name of Umm Habibah, wife of the Prophet)

Rand رند
■ Tree of good scent

Rāniyah رانية
■ Gazing

Raqībah رقيبة
■ Guardian, Supervisor

Rāshidah راشدة
■ Rightly-guided

Rashīdah رشيدة
■ Conscious, Pious

Rashīqah رشيقة
■ Elegant, Graceful

Rāsikhah راسخة
■ Firmly established, Deeply rooted (in knowledge)

Ra'ūm رؤوم
■ Loving, Tender

Rawāḥ رواح
■ Rest, Repose

Rawḍah روضة
■ Garden (in Paradise)

Rāwiyah راوية
■ Narrator, Reciter

Rayḥānah ريحانة
■ Aromatic sweet basil; (Wife of Prophet Muhammad)

Riḍwānah رضوانة
■ Pleasure, Acceptance

Rif'ah رفئة
■ Harmony, Love

Rīmah ريمة
■ Gazelle, White antelope

Rūḥānīyah روحانية
■ Spiritual

Rūḥīyah روحية
■ Spiritual

Rukān ركان
■ Steady, Confident

Ruqayyah رقية
■ Name of Prophet's daughter

Rushdā رشدى
■ Most Rightly Guided

Rushdīyah رشدية
■ Rightly guided

Ruwā' رواء
■ Prettiness

Ruwaydah رويدة
■ Walking gently

S

Sabā سبا
Queen of Sheba

Ṣabāḥ صباح
Morning, Dawn

Ṣabīḥah صبيحة
■ Beautiful, Graceful

Ṣābirah صابرة
■ Patient, Perseverent

Ṣabbūrah صبورة
■ Very Patient, Enduring

Sa'diyah سعدية
■ Fortunate; Good Fortune

Ṣādiqah صادقة
■ Truthful, Sincere

Ṣafā' صفاء
■ Purity of Mind, Clarity

Ṣafīyah صفية
■ Pure, Serene; (Wife of the Prophet Muhammad)

Saḥar سحر
■ Early Morning, Dawn

Sahlah سهلة
■ Smooth, Soft, Fluent

Ṣā'ibah صائبة
■ Straight, Pertinent

Sa'īdah سعيدة
■ Happy

Ṣā'imah صائمة
■ Fasting

Sājidah ساجدة
■ Prostrating to God

Sakīnah سكينة
■ Tranquility, Peace of Mind

Ṣāliḥah صالحة
■ Righteous, Devout

Sālimah سالمة
■ Sound

Salīmah سليمة
■ Safe, Sound, Healthy

Salmā سلمى
■ Peaceful

Salwā سلوى
■ Solace, Comfort, Quail

Salwah سلوة
■ Solace, Comfort

Samāḥ سماح
■ Generosity

Samar سمر
■ Evening Conversation

Samīḥah سميحة
■ Generous

Ṣamīmah صميمة
■ True, Sincere, Genuine

Samīrah سميرة
■ Lively Conversationalist, Jovial Companion

Sāmiyah سامية
■ Elevated, Lofty

Sanā' سناء
■ Resplendence, Brilliance

Sārah سارة
■ Pure, Happy (Wife of Prophet Ibrahim)

Sarīrah سريرة
■ Mind, Heart, Soul

Sawdah سودة
■ Proper Name (Wife of the Prophet Muhammad)

Shadhā شذى
■ Aromatic

Shafīqah شفيقة
■ Compassionate, Tender

Shāhidah شاهدة
■ Witness

Shahīdah شهيدة
■ Martyr

Shahīrah شهيرة
■ Renowned

Shā'irah شاعرة
■ Poetess

Shākirah شاكرة
■ Thankful, Grateful

Shakūrah شكورة
■ Grateful, Very Thankful

Shāmilah شاملة
■ Complete, Comprehensive

Shamīmah شميمة
■ Scent, Flavour

Shaqīqah شقيقة
■ Sister, Real Sister

Sharīfah شريفة
■ Honoured, Distinguished, Noble

Shaybah شيبة
■ A variety of Artemisia

Shaymā' شيماء
■ Proper Name (Daughter of Halimah)

Shifā' شفاء
■ Healing

Shukrīyah شكرية
■ Of Thanks, Thanksgiving

Ṣiddiqah صديقة
■ Strictly veracious, Honest

Su'ād سعاد
■ Good fortune

Ṣudāqah صداقة
■ Friend; Friendly

Suhā سها
■ Name of a Star

Suhaylah سهيلة
■ Smooth

Suhaymah سهيمة
■ Small Arrow

Sulṭānah سلطانة
■ Sultana

Sulāfah سلافة
■ Choicest

Sumayyah سمية
■ Proper Name (The first martyr in the cause of Islam)

T

Tabassum تبسم
Smile; Happiness

Ṭāhirah طاهرة
Pure, Chaste (Epithet of Khadijah, wife of the Prophet)

Taḥīyah تحية
Greeting, Cheer

Taḥsīn تحسين
■ Praise, Beautification

Taqīyah تقية
■ Godfearing, Devout

Ta'sīyah تأسية
■ Consolation, Comfort

Tasnīm تسنيم
■ Fountain of Paradise

Tawfīqah توفيقة
■ Success, Prosperity

Taysir تيسير
■ Felicitation

Ṭayyibah طيبة
■ Good, Pleasant, Agreeable

Thābitah ثابتة
■ Fixed Star; Firm

Thamīnah ثمينة
■ Precious, Generous

Thanā' ثناء
■ Thankfulness, Praise

Tharā' ثراء
■ Wealth

Tharwah ثروة
■ Wealth

Thurayyā ثريا
■ Star Pleiades

Tumādur تماضر
■ Brilliant Whiteness (Real name of Al-Khansa')

U

Ulfah ألفة
Friendship, Love, Harmony

Umāmah أمامة
- Proper Name (Name of grand daughter of the Prophet)

Umaymah أميمة
- Young Mother (Name of mother of Zaynab, wife of the Prophet)

Umm Kulthūm أم كلثوم
- Proper Name (Daughter of the Prophet)

'Urwah عروة
- Support, Handhold (Description of 'A'ishah by the Prophet)

'Uẓmā عظمى
- Greatest

W

Waddīyah ودية
- Amicable, Friendly

Wadīdah وديدة
- Attached, Devoted

Wafā' وفاء
- Faithfulness, Loyalty

Wāfiyah وافية
- Faithful, Loyal

Wafīyah وفية
- Loyalty, Faithfulness

Wāfiqah وافقة
- Successful

Wāhibah واهبة
- Giver

Waḥīdah وحيدة
- Exclusive, Unique

Wājidah واجدة
- Finder, Excited

Wājihah واجهة
- Eminent, Distinguished

Walīdah وليدة
- Newborn

Walīyah ولية
- Friend

Wardah وردة
- Rose

Wārithah وارثة
- Heiress

Waṣīlah وصيلة
- Inseparable Friend

Wasīmah وسيمة
- Graceful, Pretty

Widād وداد
- Love, Friendship

Wiṣāl وصال
- Communion in Love

Yasmīn ياسمين
- Jasmine Flower

Yumnā يمنى
- On the Right, Fortunate

Yusrā يسرى
- Most Prosperous

Z

Ẓāfirah ظافرة
- Victorious, Successful

Zāhidah زاهدة
- Ascetic, Self-denying

Zāhirah زاهرة
- Outstanding, Distinguished, Radiant

Zahīrah زهيرة
- Supporter

Zahrā' زهراء
- Radiant, Resplendent

Zahrah زهرة
- Flower, Blossom; Splendour

Zā'idah زائدة
- Increasing, Growing

Za'īmah زعيمة
- Leader

Zakīyah زكية
- Pure, Chaste

Zarqā' زرقاء
- Bluish Green (eyes)

Zaynab زينب
- Proper Name (Name of the Prophet's Daughter)

Zaytūn زيتون
- Olive

Zaytūnah زيتونة
- An Olive

Zīnah زينة
- Adornment; Beauty

Zubaydah زبيدة
- Cream of the crop; Radiant

Zuharah زهرة
- The Planet Venus

Zuhrah زهرة
- Brilliance, Brightness

MALE NAMES

ATTRIBUTES

Names beginning with ʻAbd and followed by one of the attributes of God. These attributes are not presented in alphabetical order but follows the particular order in which they are traditionally learnt or recited.

ʻAbdurRaḥmān عبد الرحمن
■ Servant of the Beneficent

ʻAbdurRaḥīm عبد الرحيم
■ Servant of the Merciful

ʻAbdulMalik عبد الملك
■ Servant of the Sovereign

ʻAbdulQuddūs عبد القدوس
■ Servant of the Holy

ʻAbdusSalām عبد السلام
■ Servant of the Author of Safety

ʻAbdulMu'min عبد المؤمن
■ Servant of the Giver of Peace

ʻAbdulMuhaymin عبد المهيمن
■ Servant of the Protector

ʻAbdulʻAzīz عبد العزيز
■ Servant of the Mighty

ʻAbdulJabbār عبد الجبار
■ Servant of the Compeller

ʻAbdulMutakabbir عبد المتكبر
■ Servant of the Majestic

ʻAbdulKhāliq عبد الخالق
■ Servant of the Creator

ʻAbdulBāri' عبد البارى
■ Servant of the Maker

ʻAbdulMuṣawwir عبد المصور
■ Servant of the Fashioner

ʻAbdulGhaffār عبد الغفار
■ Servant of the Great Forgiver

ʻAbdulQahhār عبد القهار
■ Servant of the Dominant

ʻAbdulWahhāb عبد الوهاب
■ Servant of the Bestower

ʻAbdurRazzāq عبد الرزاق
■ Servant of the Sustainer

ʻAbdulFattāḥ عبد الفتاح
■ Servant of the Reliever, the Judge

ʻAbdulʻAlīm عبد العليم
■ Servant of the All-Knowing

ʻAbdulBāsiṭ عبد الباسط
■ Servant of the Withholder, the Enlarger

ʻAbdulKhāfiḍ عبد الخافض
■ Servant of the Pleaser

ʻAbdurRāfiʻ عبد الرافع
■ Servant of the One who Elevates

ʻAbdulMuʻizz عبد المعز
■ Servant of the Giver of Might and Glory

ʻAbdulSamīʻ عبد السميع
■ Servant of the All-Hearing

ʻAbdulBaṣīr عبد البصير
■ Servant of the All-Seeing

ʻAbdulḤakam عبد الحكم
■ Servant of the Judge

ʻAbdulʻAdal عبد العدل
■ Servant of the Just

‘AbdulLaṭīf عبد اللطيف
■ Servant of the Kind, the Gracious

‘AbdulKhabīr عبد الخبير
■ Servant of the Aware, Knower of all things

‘AbdulḤalīm عبد الحليم
■ Servant of the Clement, the Forbearing

‘Abdul‘Aẓīm عبد العظيم
■ Servant of the Magnificent

‘AbdulGhafūr عبد الغفور
■ Servant of the Forgiving

‘AbdushShakūr عبد الشكور
■ Servant of the Appreciative

‘Abdul‘Alīy عبد العلى
■ Servant of the High, the Sublime

‘AbdulKabīr عبد الكبير
■ Servantt of the Great

‘AbdulḤafīẓ عبد الحفيظ
■ Servant of the Preserver

‘AbdulMuqīt عبد المقيت
■ Servant of the Sustainer

‘AbdulḤasīb عبد الحسيب
■ Servant of the Reckoner

‘AbdulKarīm عبد الكريم
■ Servant of the Bountiful, the Gracious

‘AbdulRaqīb عبد الرقيب
■ Servant of the Watchful

‘AbdulMujīb عبد المجيب
■ Servant of the One who Responds

‘AbdulWasi عبد الواسع
■ Servant of the All-Embracing

‘AbdulḤakīm عبد الحكيم
■ Servant of the Wise

‘AbdulWadūd عبد الودود
■ Servant of the Loving

‘AbdulMajīd عبد المجيد
■ Servant of the Glorious

‘AbdulBā‘ith عبد الباعث
■ Servant of the One Who Resurrects

‘AbdushShahīd عبد الشهيد
■ Servant of the Witness

‘AbdulḤaqq عبد الحق
■ Servant of the Truth

‘AbdulWakīl عبد الوكيل
■ Servant of the Helper

‘AbdulQawīy عبد القوي
■ Servant of the Strong

‘AbdulMatīn عبد المتين
■ Servant of the Firm

‘AbdulWalīy عبد الولي
■ Servant of the Protecting Friend

‘AbdulḤamīd عبد الحميد
■ Servant of the Praiseworthy, the Ever-praised

‘AbdulMuḥṣīy عبد المحصى
■ Servant of the Reckoner

‘AbdulMubdi’ عبد المبدئ
■ Servant of the Originator

‘AbdulMu‘īd عبد المعيد
■ Servant of the Reproducer

‘AbdulMuḥyi عبد المحي
■ Servant of the Restorer, the Giver of Life

‘AbdulḤayy عبد الحي
■ Servant of the Ever-living

‘AbdulQayyūm عبد القيوم
■ Servant of the Self-Subsisting

‘AbdulWājid عبد الواجد
■ Servant of the Perceiver

‘AbdulMājid عبد الماجد
■ Servant of the Illustrious

‘AbdulWāḥid عبد الواحد
■ Servant of the One

‘AbdulAḥad عبد الأحد
■ Servant of the One

‘AbdusṢamad عبد الصمد
■ Servant of the Independent

‘AbdulQādir عبد القادر
■ Servant of the Capable, the Powerful

‘AbduzẒāhir عبد الظاهر
■ Servant of the Manifest

‘AbdulBāṭin عبد الباطن
Servant of the Hidden

‘AbdulWālīy عبد الوالي
Servant of the Protector

‘AbdulMuta‘āl عبد المتعالي
Servant of the Exalted

‘AbdulBarr عبد البر
Servant of the Righteous

‘AbdutTawwāb عبد التواب
Servant of the Relenting

‘AbdulMun‘im عبد المنعم
Servant of the Benefactor

‘AbdulMuntaqim عبد المنتقم
Servant of the Avenger

‘Abdul‘Afūw عبد العفو
Servant of the Forgiver

‘AbdurRa’ūf عبد الرؤوف
Servant of the Compassionate

‘AbdurRabb عبد الرب
Servant of the Sustainer

‘AbdulMuqsiṭ عبد المقسط
Servant of the Equitable

‘AbdulJāmi‘ عبد الجامع
Servant of the Collector

‘AbdulGhanī عبد الغني
Servant of the Self-Sufficient

‘AbdulMughnī عبد المغني
Servant of the Enricher

‘AbdulMu‘ṭī عبد المعطي
Servant of the Bestower

‘AbdunNāfi‘ عبد النافع
Servant of the Propitious

‘AbdunNūr عبد النور
Servant of the (Source of) Light

‘AbdulHādi عبد الهادى
Servant of the Guide

‘AbdulBadī‘ عبد البديع
Servant of the Originator

‘AbdulBāqi عبد الباقي
Servant of the Everlasting

‘AbdulWārith عبد الوارث
Servant of the Heir

‘AbdurRashīd عبد الرشيد
Servant of the Guide to the Right Path

‘AbduṣṢabūr عبد الصبور
Servant of the Patient

Names of Prophets Mentioned in the Qur'an

Ādam	آدم
Alyasa'	اليسع
Ayyūb	أيوب
Dāwūd	داوود
Dhu-l Kifl	ذوالكفل
Hārūn	هارون
Hūd	هود
Ibrāhīm	إبراهيم
Idrīs	إدريس
Ilyās	إلياس
'Imrān	عمران
'Īsā	عيسى
Ishāq	إسحاق
Ismā'īl	إسماعيل
Lūṭ	لوط
Muḥammad	محمد
Mūsā	موسى
Nūḥ	نوح
Sāliḥ	صالح
Shu'ayb	شعيب
Sulaymān	سليمان
'Uzayr	عزير
Yaḥyā	يحي
Ya'qūb	يعقوب
Yūnus	يونس
Yūsuf	يوسف
Zakarīyā	زكريا

Names of Prophet Muhammad

Aḥmad أحمد
■ Commendable, Praiseworthy

Āmir آمر
■ Commander

Amīn أمين
■ Trustworthy

Bashīr بشير
■ Bringer of Good News

Jawwād جواد
■ Generous

Ḥāmid حامد
■ Praising

Ḥabibullāh حبيب الله
■ Beloved of God

Khātim خاتم
■ Last, Seal

Khalīl خليل
■ Friend

Daa' دا ع
■ Inviter

Sirāj سراج
■ Lamp

Sayyid سيد
■ Chief, Leader

Shāfi شافيء
■ Healing

Shāhid شاهد
■ Witness

Shahīd شهيد
■ Witness

Shahīr شهير
■ Famous

Ṣādiq صادق
■ Truthful

Ṣafiy-Allah صفى الله
■ The pure one of God

Ṭayyib طيب
■ Good

'Ādil عادل
■ Just

'Āqib عاقب
■ End, Goal

'Abdullāh عبد الله
■ Servant of God

Fātiḥ فاتح
■ Opener, Conqueror

Qāsim قاسم
■ Distributor

Qarīb قريب
■ Near, Close

Ma'mūn مأمون
■ Trusted

Mubashshir مبشر
■ Spreader of Good News

Mubīn مبين
■ Evident

Matīn متين
■ Firm

Mujtabā مجتبى
■ Selected

Muḥarram محرم
■ Sacred

Muḥammad محمد
■ Praiseworthy, Commendable

Maḥmūd محمود
■ Praiseworthy

Mad'ū مدعو
■ Called

Mudhakkir مذكر
■ Reminder

Murtaḍā مرتضى
■ Agreeable

Mashhūd مشهود
■ Attested, Proven

Muṣaddiq مصدق
■ One Who attests to the Truth

Muṣṭafā مصطفى
■ Chosen

Muṭahhar مطهر
■ Purifier

Muṭī' مطيع
■ Obedient

Ma'lūm معلوم
■ Known

Muqtaṣid مقتصد
■ Intelligent

Mukarram مكرم
■ Honoured

Munajj منج
■ Rescuer

Manṣūr منصور
■ Victorious

Munīr منير
■ Radiant

Mahdī مهدى
■ Guided

Nāh ناه
■ Prohibitor

Nadhīr نذير
■ Warner

Hādī هادى
■ Guide

A

Abān أبان
- Old Arabic Name

‘Abbās عباس
- Description of a Lion; (Uncle of the Prophet)

‘Abbūd عبود
- Worshipper

‘Abdullāh عبد الله
- Servant of God

‘Ābid عابد
- Worshipper

Abū al-Khayr أبوالخير
- One Who does good

Abū Bakr أبوبكر
- Companion of the Prophet

Adham أدهم
- Black

Adīb أديب
- Scholar, Literateur; Refined

‘Ādil عادل
- Just, Honest

‘Adīl عديل
- Equal

‘Adnān عدنان
- Ancestor of North Arabians

Afḍal أفضل
- Better, Excellent

‘Affān عفان
- Modest

‘Afīf عفيف
- Chaste, Modest

Aḥmad أحمد
- More Laudable, Praiseworthy (Epithet of Prophet Muhammad)

Aḥsan أحسن
- Better

Ajmal أجمل
- More Beautiful

Ajwad أجود
- More Generous

Akbar أكبر
- Greater, Bigger

Akīd أكيد
- Certain, Sure, Firm

‘Ākif عاكف
- Attached, Intent

Akmal أكمل
- More Complete

Akram أكرم
- More Generous

‘Alā’ علاء
- Nobility, Excellence

‘Alā’uddīn علاء الدين
- Excellence of the Faith

'Alī علي
■ Excellent, Noble, Sublime

'Ālim عالم
■ Man of Learning

'Allāl علال
■ Comforter

Alṭaf ألطف
■ More delicate, More gracious

Amān أمان
■ Security, Safety, Protection

Āmil أمل
■ Hopeful

Amīn أمين
■ Reliable, Trustworthy, Custodian

Amīr أمير
■ Ruler, Prince, Commander

'Āmir عامر
■ Prosperous, Civilised, Settled

Amjad أمجد
■ More Glorious, More Illustrious

'Ammār عمار
■ Builder, Constructer

'Amr عمرو
■ Old Arabic Name

Anas أنس
■ Affection, Love

Anīq أنيق
■ Neat, Elegant

Anīs أنيس
■ Close Companion; Genial

'Antar عنتر
■ Hero in a story of chivalry

Anwar أنور
■ More Radiant, Beautiful

'Āqil عاقل
■ Sensible, Discerning, Intelligent

'Aqīl عقيل
■ The Best, the Pick

'Arafāt عرفات
■ Gathering place of pilgrims – Symbol of Unity

Araj أرج
■ Fragrance, Sweet Smell

'Ārif عارف
■ Acquainted, Devotee

'Arīf عريف
■ Knowing, Expert

Arīj أريج
■ Fragrant, Sweet-smelling

Arshad أرشد
■ Better Guided, Honest

Arqam أرقم
■ Writer, the Best Recorder (Companion of the

Arwaḥ أروح
■ More Delicate, More Gracious

Asad أسد
■ Lion

As'ad أسعد
■ Happier

Ashraf أشرف
■ Most Noble, Honourable

Aṣīl أصيل
■ Original, Authentic, Genuine

'Āṣim عاصم
■ Protector, Guardian

'Askarī عسكري
■ Soldier

Aslam أسلم
■ Safer, Sounder

'Aṭā' عطاء
■ Gift, Favour

'Aṭā'ullāh عطاء الله
■ Gift of God

Athīr أثير
■ Favoured, Preferred

‘Āṭif عاطف
■ Compassionate, Affectionate

‘Āṭir عاطر
■ Fragrant, Aromatic

‘Aṭṭār عطار
■ Perfumer

‘Awaḍ عوض
■ Reward, Compensation

‘Awn عون
■ Help, Support

Ayman أيمن
■ On the Right, Fortunate

A‘ẓam أعظم
■ Greatest

Aẓfar أظفر
■ Winner, Most Victorious

Azhar أزهر
■ Shining, Radiant

‘Azīm عزيم
■ Determined

‘Aẓmat عظمة
■ Grandeur

‘Azzām عزام
■ Determined, Resolved

B

Badr بدر
Full Moon

Badruddīn بدر الدين
Full moon of the Faith

Bahā’ بهاء
Brilliance, Beauty

Bahāuddīn بهاء الله
■ The Brilliance of the Faith

Bahī بهي
■ Splendid, Brilliant

Bāhir باهر
■ Dazzling, Brilliant

Bakr بكر
■ First born

Bakūr بكور
Precocious

Bāligh بالغ
■ Clear, Eloquent

Barakat بركة
■ Blessing

Barī’ بريء
■ Innocent

Barrāq براق
■ Shining, Lustrous

Bashshar بشار
■ Bringer of Glad Tidings

Bashīr بشير
■ Bringer of Good News

Bāsil باسل
■ Brave

Bāsim باسم
■ Smiling

Bassām بسام
■ Smiling

Baṭal بطل
■ Brave; Champion

Bilāl بلال
■ Companion of the Prophet

Bishr بشر
■ Joy

Burhān برهان
■ Evidence, Proof

Burhānuddīn برهان الدين
■ Proof of the Faith

D

Dalīl دليل
Guide, Conductor

Damīr ضمير
Conscience

Dhahab ذهب
Gold

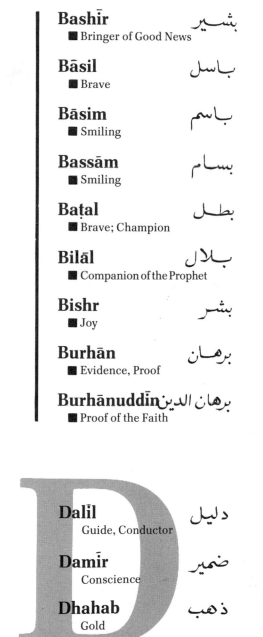

Dhahabī ذهبى
■ Golden, Precious

Dhakī ذكى
■ Intelligent, Clever

Dhākir ذاكر
■ One who remembers God

Dhu-l Fiqār ذوالفقار
■ Name of the Prophet's Sword

Ḍiyā' ضياء
■ Light, Splendour

Ḍiyā'uddīn ضياء الدين
■ Brightness of the Faith

F

Fādī' فادىء
Redeemer

Fāḍil فاضل
Outstanding, Virtuous, Erudite

Faḍīl فضيل
Eminent, Distinguished

Faḍl فضل
■ Reward, Favour

Faḍlullāh فضل الله
■ Bounty of God

Fahd فهد
■ Tiger, Lynx

Fahīm فهيم
■ Intelligent, Discerning

Fā'iq فائق
■ Surpassing, Excellent

Fā'iz فائز
■ Victorious

Fākhir فاخر
■ Excellent, Proud

Fakhr فخر
■ Pride, Glory

Fakhrī فخرى
■ Glorious, Proud

Fakhruddīn فخرالدين
■ Pride of the Religion

Falāḥ فلاح
■ Success

Faqīh فقيه
■ Understanding; Expert, Jurist

Faqīr فقير
■ Poor (in relation to God)

Faraḥ فرح
■ Happy, Glad

Farḥat فرحة
■ Joy, Mirth

Farīd فريد
■ Unique

Farīh فريه
■ Lively, Comely

Fāris فارس
■ Horseman, Knight

Fārūq فاروق
■ He who distinguishes Truth from falsehood

Faṣīḥ فصيح
■ Eloquent

Fatḥ فتح
■ Initiation, Liberation

Fatḥī فتحي
■ Of Liberation

Fātiḥ فاتح
■ Victor, Conquerer

Fātin فاتن
■ Clever, Fascinating

Fattān فتان
■ Charming, Bright

Fawwāz فواز
■ Successful

Fawz فوز
■ Success, Triumph

Fawzī فوزى
■ Successful

Fayḍ فيض
■ Abundance, Favour

Fayṣal فيصل
- Decisive

Fayyāḍ فياض
- Generous, Liberal

Fidā' فداء
- Sacrifice, Ransom

Firās فراس
- Perspicacity

Firāsah فراسة
- Perspicacity

Fu'ād فؤاد
- Heart

Furqān فرقان
- Evidence, Proof

Furūkh فروخ
- Sprout, Shoot, Young (bird)

G

Ghālib غالب
- Overpowering; Conqueror

Ghānim غانم
- Successful

Ghawth غوث
- Help, Succour

Ghāzī غازى
- Conqueror, Warrior

Ghiyāth غياث
- Aid, Succour

Ghiyāthuddīn غياث الدين
- Helper of the Faith

Ghufrān غفران
- Forgiveness

H

Ḥabīb حبيب
- Beloved

Hābīl هابيل
- Abel

Hādī' هادىء
- Calm, Tranquil

Hādī هادى
- Guiding to the Right; Guide

Ḥāfiẓ حافظ
- Protector, Guardian

Ḥafīẓ حفيظ
- Attentive, Heedful

Ḥākim حاكم
- Ruler, Sovereign

Ḥalīf حليف
- Ally, Confederate

Ḥamas حمس
- Enthusiasm, Fervour

Ḥamdī, حمدى
- Of Praise, Commendation

Ḥāmid حامد
- Praising (God), Commendable

Ḥamīm حميم
- Close Friend

Ḥammād حماد
- Praising (God)

Ḥammūd حمود
- Thankful, Grateful

Ḥamzah حمزة
- Lion (Uncle of the Prophet)

Hānī' هانئ
- Joyful, Happy

Ḥanīf حنيف
- Upright, True Believer

Ḥannān حنان
- Compassionate

Ḥaqqānī حقانى
- Correct, Right, Proper

Ḥāris حارس
- Vigilant; Guardian, Protector

Ḥārith حارث
- Ploughman, Tiller (Old Arabic Name)

Ḥasan حسن
■ Handsome, Good

Hāshim هاشم
■ One who breaks (bread) to distribute, Generous; (Great Grandfather of the Prophet)

Ḥasīb حسيب
■ Respected, Esteemed, Noble

Ḥaṣīf حصيف
■ Endowed with sound judgment

Ḥāsin حاسن
■ Final, Decisive

Ḥasīn حسين
■ Handsome

Ḥassān حسان
■ Very Handsome

Ḥātim حاتم
■ Judge

Ḥayyān حيان
■ Lively, Energetic

Ḥāzim حازم
■ Discreet, Prudent

Ḥaẓīẓ حظيظ
■ Fortunate

Hilāl هلال
■ Crescent

Ḥilmī حلمي
■ Wise

Hishām هشام
■ Generosity

Ḥubaab حباب
■ Friendship, Aim

Ḥudhayfah حذيفة
■ Old Arabic Name

Ḥulayl حليل
■ Old Arabic Name

Ḥusām حسام
■ Sword

Ḥusāmuddīn حسام الدين
■ The Sword of the Faith

Ḥusayn حسين
■ Handsome, Beautiful

Ḥusnī حسني
■ Good, Handsome

I

Iftikhār إفتخار
Honour, Glory

Iḥsān إحسان
Benevolence, Sincerity

I'jāz إعجاز
Miracle, Astonishment

Ikhlāṣ إخلاص
■ Sincerity, Purity

Ikrām إكرام
■ Esteem, Veneration, Respect

Ikrimah عكرمة
■ Proper Name

'Imād عماد
■ Support, Pillar, Confidence

'Imāduddin عماد الدين
■ The Pillar of Faith

Imām إمام
■ Leader

Imdād إمداد
■ Help, Support

Imtiyāz إمتياز
■ Privilege, Distinction

In'ām انعام
■ Reward, Grant

'Ināyah عناية
■ Concern, Attention

Inṣāf انصاف
■ Justice, Equity

Iqbāl اقبال
■ Responsiveness

'Irfān عرفان
■ Perception

Irshād ارشاد
■ Guidance, Guiding hand

'Iṣām عصام
■ Safeguard, Bond

Ishfāq اشفاق
■ Compassion, Tenderness

Isrār اسرار
■ Persistence, Perseverance

I'timād اعتماد
■ Trust, Faith

'Izzuddīn عزالدين
■ Might of the Faith

J

Jābir جابر
Restorer, Consoler

Jadwa جدوة
Gift, Present

Ja'far جعفر
Stream, Rivulet (Cousin, Companion of the Prophet)

Jah جاه
■ Rank, Dignity

Jalāl جلال
■ Glory, Grandeur

Jalāluddīn جلال الدين
■ Glory of the Faith

Jalīl جليل
■ Exalted, Fine

Jamāl جمال
■ Beauty, Grace

Jamāluddīn جمال الدين
■ Beauty of the Faith

Jamīl جميل
■ Beautiful, Lovely, Graceful

Jamūḥ جموح
■ Defiant

Jawād جواد
■ Liberal, Generous

Jawhar جوهر
■ Gem, Jewel

Jawharī جوهري
■ Intrinsic, Essential (nature)

Jibrān جبران
■ Reward

Jibrīl جبريل
■ Archangel Gabriel

Jihād جهاد
■ Struggle

Junayd جنيد
■ (Little) Fighter, Warrior

K

Kafīl كفيل
Guarantor, Responsible

Kalīm كليم
Orator

Kamāl كمال
Perfection, Completeness

Kāmil كامل
■ Complete, Perfect

Karāmah كرامة
■ Nobility, Generosity Miracle

Kāshif كاشف
■ Discoverer

Kasīb كسيب
■ Winner, Provider

Kathīr كثير
■ Ample, Abundance

Kawkab كوكب
■ Planet

Kāẓim كاظم
■ Controller, Restrainer of anger

Khabīr خبير
■ Experienced, Expert

Khalaf خلف
■ Heir, Successor

Khaldūn خلدون
■ Proper Name

Khālid خـــالد
- Glorious, Eternal

Khalīfah خليفـة
- Successor, Caliph

Khalīl خليـل
- Friend (Epithet of Prophet Ibrahim)

Khāliṣ خـــالص
- Pure, Clear

Khaṭīb خطيب
- Orator

Khāṭir خـــاطر
- Heart, Idea

Khayr خـــير
- Good, Benevolent

Khayrī خـــيرى
- Charitable, Beneficent

Khayruddīn خيرالدين
- Goodness of the Faith

Khayyām خيـــام
- Tentmaker

Khayyir خـــير
- Generous, Liberal

Khāzin خـــازن
- Treasurer

Khiḍr خضـر
- Guide, Leader

L

Labīb لبيب
Sensible, Intelligent, Understanding

Lā'iq لائـق
Able, Deserving

Laṭīf لطيف
Fine, Gentle, Refined

Layyin لـيـن
- Tender, Resilient

Liyāqah لـيـاقة
- Fitness, Competence

Lu'ay لأى
- Proper Name

Luqmān لقمـــان
- Name of person in the Qur'an granted wisdom by God

Luṭf لطـــف
- Kindness, Gentleness

Luṭfi لطفى
- Kind, Friendly, Gentle

Luṭfullāh لطف الله
- Kindness of God

M

Ma'ālī معـــالى
Noble, Sublime (qualities)

Madanī مــدنى
- Polished, Urbane, Civilized

Madīḥ مــديح
- Praised, Commendable

Maḥbūb محبوب
- Beloved, Dear

Mahdī مهـــدى
- Rightly guided

Maḥfūẓ محفوظ
- Preserved, Safe

Māhir مـــاهر
- Skilled

Maḥmūd محمود
- Praised, Commendable

Maḥẓūẓ محظوظ
- Fortunate

Majd مجد
- Glory, Nobility

Majdī مجدى
- Glorious, Praiseworthy

Mājid مـــاجد
- Glorious, Noble

Makīn مكين
- Strong, Firm

Malik ملك
- Sovereign, King

Malīk مليك
■ Reigning, Ruling

Mamdūḥ ممدوح
■ Commended, Praised

Ma'mūn مأمون
■ Reliable, Trustworthy

Man مان
■ Benefit

Manāẓir مناظر
■ Equal Competitor

Manṣūr منصور
■ Aided (by God, Victorious)

Maqbūl مقبول
■ Accepted, Popular

Maqṣūd مقصود
■ Proposed, Intended

Marghūb مرغوب
■ Desired, Agreeable

Mariḥ مريح
■ Joyful, Lively

Ma'rūf معروف
■ Known, Accepted

Marwān مروان
■ Proper Name

Marzūq مرزوق
■ Blessed, Fortunate

Mashkūr مشكور
■ Thankful, Praiseworthy

Masrūr مسرور
■ Happy, Glad

Mas'ūd مسعود
■ Happy

Ma'sūm معصوم
■ Innocent

Mawdūd مودود
■ Loving, Attached

Maymūn ميمون
■ Fortunate, Blessed

Maysarah ميسرة
■ Ease, Comfort

Maẓhar مظهر
■ Manifestation, Phenomenon

Mazin مازن
■ Proper Name

Miqdam مقدام
■ Daring, Valiant

Misbah مصباح
■ Light, Lamp

Mi'yār معيار
■ Standard, Norm

Mu'ādh معاذ
■ Companion of the Prophet

Mu'ammar معمر
■ Senior

Ma'awwin معون
■ Helper, Assistant

Mu'ayyad مؤيد
■ Supported

Mu'aẓẓam معظم
■ Respected, Magnified

Mubārak مبارك
■ Blessed, Fortunate, Auspicious

Mubīn مبين
■ Clear, Evident

Mudabbir مدبر
■ Prudent, Manager

Muddaththir مدثر
■ Covered (Epithet of the Prophet)

Mufīd مفيد
■ Useful, Favourable

Mufliḥ مفلح
■ Lucky; One who prospers

Mughīth مغيث
■ Helper, Succourer

Muḥibb محب
■ Loving

Muḥsin محسن
■ Benevolent; Benefactor

Muhtadī مهتدى
■ Rightly guided

Mu'īn معين
■ Helper

Mu'īnuddīn معين الدين
■ Helper of the Faith

Mujāhid مجاهد
■ Struggler, Fighter

Mujīr مجير
■ Protector

Mukhliṣ مخلص
■ Sincere, Devoted, Pure-hearted

Mumtāz ممتاز
■ Distinguished, Excellent

Munawwar منور
■ Enlightened, Lighted

Mundhir منذر
■ Warner

Munīb منيب
■ Repentant

Mun'im منعم
■ Generous, Benefactor

Munīr منير
■ Brilliant, Radiant

Munis منس
■ Companion, Consoler

Munṣif منصف
■ Judge, Righteous

Muntaṣir منتصر
■ Victorious, Triumphant

Muqaddas مقدس
■ Sacred

Murād مراد
■ Desired, Wanted

Murīḥ مريح
■ Restful, Soothing

Murshid مرشد
■ Guide, Spiritual Guide

Murtaḍā مرتضى
■ Satisfied, Content

Murtāḥ مرتاح
■ Content, Tranquil

Muṣ'ab مصعب
■ Name of a Companion of the Prophet

Muṣaddaq مصدق
■ Credible, Trustworthy

Muṣaddiq مصدق
■ One who attests to the Truth

Muṣāliḥ مصالح
■ Peace-maker, Mediator

Musharraf مشرف
■ Elevated, Honoured

Muṣliḥ مصلح
■ Conciliator, Reformer

Muṣṭafā مصطفى
■ Chosen (Epithet of Muhammad)

Muṭahhar مطهر
■ Pure, Immaculate

Mu'taṣim معتصم
■ Adhering to Faith

Mutawakkil متوكل
■ Relying on God

Mu'tazz معتز
■ Proud, Mighty

Muṭī' مطيع
■ Obedient

Muttaqī متقى
■ God-fearing, Pious

Muwaffaq موفق
■ Successful

Muwaḥḥid موحد
■ Professor of the Unity of God

Muẓaffar مظفر
■ Victorious, Triumphant

Muzzammil مزمل
■ One who is wrapped up (Epithet of Muhammad)

N

Nabīh نبيه
Noble, Outstanding

Nabīl نبيل
■ Noble, Generous

Nadhīr نذير
■ Warner

Nādim نادم
■ Repentant, Regretful

Nadīm نديم
■ Companion, Friend

Nāḍir نادر
■ Rare, Precious

Naḍīr نضير
■ Flourishing, Radiant, Blooming

Nafīs نفيس
■ Precious

Nāhiḍ ناهض
■ Elevated

Nā'il نائل
■ Earner, Acquirer

Na'īm نعيم
■ Tranquil; Ease, Comfort

Najā نجا
■ Useful, Beneficial

Najāh نجاة
■ Escape, Safety

Nāji' ناجئ
■ Safe

Najīb نجيب
■ Noble, Distinguished

Nājiḥ ناجح
■ Successful

Najm نجم
■ Star, Celestial body

Najmuddīn نجم الدين
■ Star of the Faith

Naqī نقي
■ Pure, Clean

Naqīb نقيب
■ Leader, Head

Nāṣif ناصف
■ Just, Equitable

Naṣīf نصيف
■ Most Just, Equitable

Nāṣiḥ ناصح
■ Counsellor, Advisor

Nāsik ناسك
■ Pious, Devotee

Nasīm نسيم
■ Breath of fresh air, Breeze

Nāsiq ناسق
■ Well ordered, Well-arranged

Nāṣir ناصر
■ Helper, Protector, Supporter

Naṣīr نصير
■ Supporter, Defender

Nāṣiruddīn ناصرالدين
■ Protector of the Faith

Naṣr نصر
■ Help, Victory

Naṣruddīn نصرالدين
■ Victory of the Faith

Naṣṣāḥ نصاح
■ Good Counsellor

Nawfal نوفل
■ Generous

Nayyār نيار
■ Brilliant, Luminous

Nazīh نزيه
■ Pure Honourable, Chaste

Nāẓim ناظم
■ Organizer, Versifier

Nāẓir ناظر
■ Observer, Supervisor

Naẓẓār نظار
■ Keen-eyed

Niḍāl نضال
■ Fight, Defence

Ni'mah نعمة
■ Blessing, Grace, Bounty

Ni'matullāh نعمة الله
■ Grace of God

Nu'mān نعمان
■ Soul, Blood (Old Arabic Name)

Nūr نور
■ Light

Nūrānī نوراني
■ Luminous

Nūrī نوری
■ Brilliant, Shining

Nūruddīn نورالدين
■ Light of the Faith

Q

Qadūm قدوم
Intrepid, Undaunted

Qāhir قاهر
Overpowering, Victorious

Qā'im قائم
Stable, Upright

Qamar قمر
■ Moon

Qamaruddīn قمرالدين
■ Moon of the Faith

Qāni' قانع
■ Satisfied

Qarār قرار
■ Rest, Firmness

Qāsim قاسم
■ Divider, Distributor (Name of a son of the Prophet)

Qays قيس
■ Firm

Qiyām قيام
■ Rising, Standing

Qudāmah قدامة
■ Courage

Qutb قطب
■ Pivot, Celebrity, Leading Personality

R

Rabāḥ رباح
Gainer

Rabī' ربيع
Spring

Rafī' رفيع
Exalted, High

Rābigh رابغ
■ Pleasant, Comfortable

Rāḍī راضی
■ Satisfied, Content

Rafā' رفاء
■ Mercy, Compassion

Rafī' رفيع
■ High, Sublime, Exquisite

Rafīq رفيق
■ Kind Friend, Ally

Rāghib راغب
■ Willing, Desirous, Desiring

Raḥīb رحيب
■ Generous

Rā'ī راعی
■ Shepherd, Steward

Rā'id رائد
■ Pioneer

Ra'īs رئيس
■ Chief, Head

Rajā' رجاء
■ Hope

Rajab رجب
■ Month of the Muslim Calendar

Rājiḥ راجح
■ Superior in Weight, Firmer

Rākin راكن
■ Respectful

Ramaḍān رمضان
Month of Fasting

Rāmiz رامز
Symbol

Raqīb رقيب
Guardian, Supervisor

Raqīq رقيق
Tender, Sensitive, Prudent

Rashād رشاد
Integrity, Maturity

Rāshid راشد
Following the right way, Righteous, Pious

Rashīd رشيد
Rightly guided

Rashīq رشيق
Elegant, Graceful

Rāsikh راسخ
Stable, Firmly Established

Ra'ūf رؤوف
Merciful, Kind, Compassionate

Rayḥān ريحان
Sweet basil

Rayyān ريان
Full, Pretty

Riḍā' رضاء
Contentment, Satisfaction

Riḍwān رضوان
Pleasure, Goodwill, Acceptance

Riyāḍ رياض
Gardens

Rūḥānī روحانى
Spiritual

Rūḥī روحى
Spiritual, of the Soul

S

Ṣabbār صبار
Very Patient

Ṣabīḥ صبيح
Handsome, Graceful

Ṣābir صابر
Patient, Enduring, Persevering

Ṣabūr صبور
Patient, Perseverant

Sa'd سعد
Felicity, Good luck

Ṣādiq صادق
Truthful, Sincere

Ṣadr صدر
Breast; Heart

Ṣadruddīn صدر الدين
Heart of the Religion

Ṣāfī صافى
Best Friend, Pure

Ṣafwān صفوان
Old Arabic Name

Sāḥir ساحر
Wakeful

Sa'īd سعيد
Happy, Fortunate

Sājid ساجد
Prostrating

Sajjād سجاد
One who prostrates much, Worshipper of God

Sakhī سخى
Generous, Liberal

Ṣalāḥ صلاح
Goodness, Righteousness

Ṣalāḥuddīn صلاح الدين
Righteousness of the Faith

Salamah سلمة
Soundness, Integrity

Salāmah سلامة
Soundness, Safety

Sālim سالم
Secure, Free

Salīm سليم
■ Safe, Sound

Ṣalmān سلمان
■ Safe

Sāmī سامى
■ Lofty

Ṣamīm صميم
■ Heart, Essence; Genuine

Samīr سمير
■ Entertaining Companion

Ṣaqr صقر
■ Falcon

Sa'ūd سعود
■ Felicities, Good Fortune

Sayfuddīn سيف الدين
■ Sword of the Faith

Sayful-l Islām سيف الإسلام
■ Sword of Islam

Shāfi' شافئ
■ Advocate, Mediator

Shafīq شفيق
■ Compassionate, Kind, Tender

Shāhid شاهد
■ Witness

Shahīd شهيد
■ Martyr, Witness

Shāhīn شاهين
■ Falcon

Shahīr شهير
■ Renowned

Shāji شجيع
■ Courageous, Brave

Shākir شاكر
■ Thankful, Grateful

Shāmil, شامل
■ Comprehensive, Complete

Shāmis شامس
■ Sunny

Shamsuddīn شمس الدين
■ The sun of the Faith

Sharaf شرف
■ Distinction, Dignity

Sharīf شريف
■ Noble, Distinguished, Honoured

Shihāb شهاب
■ Star, The Shooting Star

Shukrī شكرى
■ Thankful

Siddīq صديق
■ Veracious, Righteous

Sirāj سراج
■ Lamp, Light

Sirājuddīn سراج الدين
■ Light of the Faith

Ṣubḥī صبحى
■ Early Morning

Suhayb صهيب
■ Of Reddish hair, or complexion (Companion of the Prophet)

Suhayl سهيل
■ Easy, Smooth

Suhayr سهير
■ Proper Name

Sulāf سلاف
■ Choicest

Sulāfuddīn سلاف الدين
■ Choice of the Faith

Sulṭān سلطان
■ Power, Authority

Surūr سرور
■ Joy, Happiness

Su'ūd سعود
■ Good Luck, Rising

T

Ṭāhā طه
Proper Name

Ṭāhir طاهر
Pure, Virtuous

Taḥrīr تحرير
■ Liberation

Ṭalāl طلال
■ Admirable

Ṭalḥah طلحة
■ Companion of the Prophet

Ṭālib طالب
■ Seeker (of Knowledge) Student

Tāmir تامر
■ One who owns dates

Tanwīr تنوير
■ Enlightening

Tanzīl تنزيل
■ Revelation, Inspiration

Taqī تقى
■ God-fearing, Devout

Taslīm تسليم
■ Submission, Name of a star

Tawqīr توقير
■ Honour, Respect

Tawfīq توفيق
■ Prosperity, Success

Ṭayyib طيب
■ Good, Pleasant, Agreeable

Thābit ثابت
■ Firm, Established

Thamar ثمر
■ Fruit, Profit

Thāqib ثاقب
■ Piercing, Glistening

Ṭufayl طفيل
■ Mediator

Ṭulayb طليب
■ Proper Name (Companion of the Prophet)

U

'Ubādah عبادة
■ Proper Name

'Ubayd عبيد
■ Servant (of God)

'Ubaydullāh عبيد الله
■ Servant of God

'Ubaydah عبيدة
■ Servant of God

Ubayy أبيّ
■ Proper Name

'Umar عمر
■ Lifetime Companion of the Prophet & Second Khalifah)

'Umārah عمارة
■ Old Arabic Name

'Umayr عمير
■ Old Arabic Name

'Umrān عمران
■ Prosperity

Unays أنيس
■ Diminutive of Anas

'Uqbah عقبة
■ Old Arabic Name

'Urwah عروة
■ Hand-hold, Support

Usāmah أسامة
■ Lion (Companion of the Prophet)

Usayd أسيد
■ Little lion Companion of the Prophet

'Utbah عتبة
■ Old Arabic Name

'Uthmān عثمان
■ Companion of the Prophet & Third Khalifah

Uways أويس
■ Name of an early Muslim noted for his asceticism

W

Wāfī وافى
Faithful, Loyal

Wāfiq وافق
■ Successful

Wahb وهب
■ Giving

Wahhāj وهاج
■ Sparkling, Glowing

Wāhib واهب
■ Liberal donor

Wahīd وحيد
■ Unique, Exclusive

Wā'il وائل
■ Returning (for Shelter)

Wā'iẓ واعظ
■ Preacher

Wajāhah وجاهة
■ Esteem, Credit

Wājid واجد
■ Finder

Wajīh وجيه
■ Notable, Eminent

Walī ولي
■ Friend

Walīd وليد
■ Newborn

Walīyuddīn ولي الدين
■ Supporter of the Faith

Walīyullāh ولي الله
■ Supporter of God

Waqār وقار
■ Dignity, Sobriety

Wārith وارث
■ Heir

Waṣīl وصيل
■ Inseparable friend

Wasīm وسيم
■ Handsome, Graceful

Wathīq وثيق
■ Firm, Reliable, Confident

Wazīr وزير
■ Minister, Vizier

Y

Yamīn يمين
■ Right

Yāsīn ياسين
■ Proper Name
One of the Prophet
Muhammad's names

Yāsir ياسر
■ Wealthy
(Companion of the
Prophet)

Yazīd يزيد
■ To increase, grow,
enchance

Z

Ẓafar ظفر
■ Victory, Triumph

Ẓāfir ظافر
■ Victorious

Zāhid زاهد
■ Abstinent, Ascetic,
Devotee

Zāhir زاهر
■ Shining, Radiant,
Elevated

Ẓāhir ظاهر
■ Distinct, Conspicuous

Zā'id زائد
■ Increasing, Growing

Za'īm زعيم
■ Leader

Zakī زكي
■ Pure, Chaste

Zamān زمان
■ Time, Destiny

Ẓarīf ظريف
■ Witty

Zayyān زيان
■ Beautiful

Zayd زيد
■ Superabundant

Zayn زين
■ Beauty

Zaynu-l'Ābidīn زين العابدين
- Beauty of Worshippers (Son of Husayn, grandson of the Prophet)

Ziyād زياد
- Abundance

Zubayr زبير
- Proper Name (Companion of the Prophet)

Zuhayr زهير
- Bright